The Master's TABLE

A PASSOVER
ENCOUNTER FOR
CHRISTIANS

FIRST FRUITS OF
ZION

First Edition 2017
Printed in the United States of America

ISBN: 978-1-941534-23-6

Development: Aaron Eby and Toby Janicki
Design: First Fruits of Zion

First Fruits of Zion
US Distribution Center: PO Box 649, Marshfield, Missouri 65706-0649 USA
Phone (417) 468-2741, www.ffoz.org

Comments and questions may be sent to: feedback@ffoz.org

The Master's Table: A Passover Encounter for Christians contains an order of service to celebrate a Passover seder. For more information on this resource and other books and resources for the education and celebration of Jewish festivals please visit www.ffoz.org.

The Master's TABLE

Glad songs of salvation are in the tents of the righteous:
"The right hand of the LORD does valiantly,
The right hand of the LORD exalts,
the right hand of the LORD does valiantly!"
I shall not die, but I shall live,
and recount the deeds of the LORD.
The LORD has disciplined me severely,
but he has not given me over to death.
Open to me the gates of righteousness,
that I may enter through them
and give thanks to the LORD.

Psalm 118 : 15–19

The Master's
TABLE

INTRODUCTION

And he said to them, "I have earnestly desired to eat this Passover with you before I suffer."
(Luke 22:15)

As a faithful Jew, our Messiah Jesus celebrated Passover every year. Passover is a biblical festival celebrating the salvation of the Israelites from slavery in Egypt.

The death and resurrection of Jesus occurred at Passover. How fitting that his Hebrew name, Yeshua, means "the LORD saves!" The last meal that he ate with his disciples before his death was a Passover meal.

The bread that Yeshua called his "body" was matzah, the unleavened bread of Passover. The wine that he called his "blood" was Passover wine. Moreover, every symbol and item on the customary Passover table connects in some way with him. By celebrating Passover in honor of our Master, we re-enact this sacred moment and proclaim his death until he comes.

The Passover meal is called a seder, which means "set order." It is called this because it consists of a list of steps that ensure we accomplish all our goals for the night. A Passover guidebook such as this one is called a *Haggadah*, which means "telling." The primary purpose of the Passover Seder is to tell the story of redemption.

The Gospel of Luke tells us that Yeshua was lost and found as a boy at Passover time. His family found him in what should have been the most obvious place. He was at the Temple, sitting and learning among the rabbis of Israel. Have we also left Jesus behind in the dust? Perhaps we will encounter him again at Passover, at home among the teachers of his people.

PREPARATION FOR THE SEDER

REMOVAL OF LEAVEN

Before Passover begins, Jewish families remove all leavened food from their possession. Fluffy loaves of bread definitely have to go. But the Hebrew word for leaven, *chametz*, refers to anything made from grain and allowed to ferment, even slightly. Cookies, noodles, and certain kinds of drinks are included! For all seven days of Passover, Jewish families use matzah instead of other grain-based foods.

CANDLE LIGHTING

Jewish women typically light a set of candles at home shortly before sunset. (It is *not* customary to light candles as a part of the seder itself.)

THE SEDER PLATE

We place several different symbolic foods on a special plate or tray at the Passover table. The plate contains a small portion of each the following symbolic foods:

Zeroa (zeh-ROW-ah)
A roasted lamb shank bone
Represents the Passover lamb offering

Beitzah (bay-TSAH)
A roasted egg
Represents the festival sacrifice

Karpas (kar-POSS)
A green vegetable, typically parsley or celery
Represents the betrayal of Joseph

Charoset (hah-ROW-set)
A mushy mixture of fruit, nuts, spices, and wine
Represents mortar for building

Maror (mah-ROAR) and Chazeret (ha-ZEH-ret)
Bitter herbs, commonly Romaine lettuce and fresh horseradish. Represent the bitterness of slavery

The small portions on the seder plate are for display purposes. Additional *karpas, charoset, maror,* and *chazeret* should be at the table for each participant.

MATZAH

Matzah (plural *matzot*) is a crispy cracker-like piece of unleavened bread.

The leader uses three special *matzot*. People often set these special *matzot* in a special tray or pouch. At the table, provide at least two additional pieces of matzah for each participant.

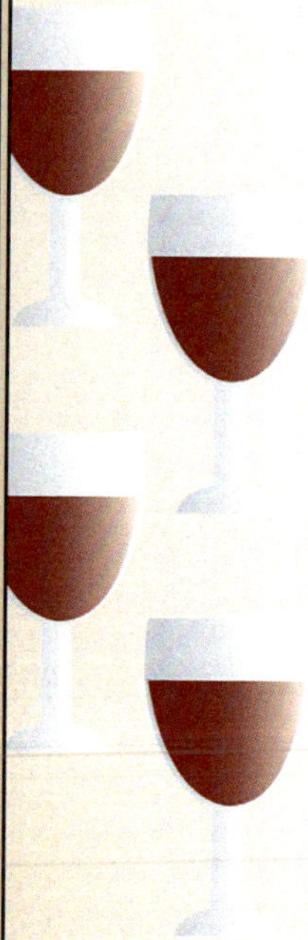

FOUR CUPS

At a traditional seder, each participant drinks four cups of wine or grape juice over the course of the evening. These correspond to the four expressions of redemption in Exodus 6:6–7:

1. **I will bring you out** from under the burdens of the Egyptians,
2. and **I will deliver you** from slavery to them,
3. and **I will redeem you** with an outstretched arm and with great acts of judgment.
4. **I will take you** to be my people.

We also set an empty place for Elijah. We fill his cup toward the end of the meal.

SALT WATER OR VINEGAR

Participants dip the *karpas* vegetable before eating. Red wine vinegar was used in ancient times. Using salt water is a more common custom in modern times.

A FESTIVE MEAL

While matzah and bitter herbs are delicious, they are not the main course. A Passover Seder includes a full holiday meal. The menu varies and can include things such as fish, meat, vegetables, and dessert. Be sure to avoid anything made from grains (unless it was made from matzah).

HAND WASHING

At two points during the seder, it is customary to rinse the hands in a ceremonial manner. This practice commemorates the priestly purity rites in the days of the Temple. If you include this in your seder, you may choose to have the leader demonstrate it or have everyone participate.

STEPS OF THE SEDER

It is customary to begin the seder by reciting the fifteen standard steps, often to a cheerful tune.

① **KADDESH** The Prayer of Sanctification	② **URCHATZ** Hand Washing
③ **KARPAS** Dip the Parsley	④ **YACHATZ** Break the Matzah
⑤ **MAGGID** Tell the Story	⑥ **ROCHTZAH** Second Washing
⑦ **MOTZI** The Blessing for Bread	⑧ **MATZAH** Eating Matzah
⑨ **MAROR** Bitter Herbs	⑩ **KORECH** Matzah and Bitter Herbs Together
⑪ **SHULCHAN ORECH** The Meal Is Served	
⑫ **TZAFUN** Eating the Hidden Matzah	⑬ **BARECH** Giving Thanks for the Meal
⑭ **HALLEL** Psalms of Praise	⑮ **NIRTZAH** Conclusion

LEADER: And when the hour came, he reclined at table, and the apostles with him. And he said to them, "I have earnestly desired to eat this Passover with you before I suffer. For I tell you I will not eat it until it is fulfilled in the kingdom of God." (Luke 22:14–16)

① KADDESH

THE PRAYER OF SANCTIFICATION

Each time you pour a cup, do not pour your own but have someone else pour it for you. Pour the first cup now.

LEADER: And he took a cup, and when he had given thanks he said, "Take this, and divide it among yourselves. For I tell you that from now on I will not drink of the fruit of the vine until the kingdom of God comes." (Luke 22:17–18)

LEADER: We thank you, our Father, for the holy vine of your servant David that you made known to us through your servant Yeshua. Yours is the glory forever.

LEADER: Blessed are you, O LORD, our God, King of the universe, who creates the fruit of the vine.

*Baruch attah ADONAI elo·**hei**·nu, **me**·lech ha'olam, borei pri ha·**ga**·fen.*

PARTICIPANTS: Amen.

LEADER: Blessed are you, O LORD, our God, King of the universe, who has lovingly given us appointed times for joy and festivals for gladness. You gave us the Festival of *Matzot*, the season of freedom, as a time of holiness and as a remembrance of the exodus from Egypt. Blessed are you, O LORD, who sanctifies Israel and the seasons.

PARTICIPANTS: Amen.

LEADER: Blessed are you, O LORD, our God, King of the universe, who has given us life, sustained us, and let us arrive at this season.

PARTICIPANTS: Amen.

Lean to the left as you drink the first cup.

② URCHATZ

THE HAND WASHING

Rinse the hands in the traditional manner.

③ KARPAS

DIP THE PARSLEY

All participants take a piece of parsley or celery and dip it into saltwater or red wine vinegar.

LEADER: Blessed are you, O LORD, our God, King of the universe, who creates the fruit of the ground.

*Baruch attah ADONAI elo·**hei**·nu, **me**·lech ha'olam,*
borei pri ha'adamah.

PARTICIPANTS: Amen.

Eat the parsley.

LEADER: When it was evening, he reclined at table with the twelve. And as they were eating, he said, "Truly, I say to you, one of you will betray me." And they were very sorrowful and began to say to him one after another, "Is it I, Lord?" He answered, "He who has dipped his hand in the dish with me will betray me. The Son of Man goes as it is written of him, but woe to that man by whom the Son of Man is betrayed! It would have been better for that man if he had not been born." Judas, who would betray him, answered, "Is it I, Rabbi?" He said to him, "You have said so." (Matthew 26:20–25)

④ YACHATZ

BREAK THE MATZAH

Remove the middle piece of matzah and break it in two. Put the smaller part back between the two whole matzot. The larger piece is called the afikoman. Wrap the afikoman and set it aside until after the meal.

⑤ MAGGID

TELL THE STORY

Lift the matzot.

LEADER: This is the bread of affliction that the Israelites ate in Egypt. Let all who are hungry come and eat! Let all who are needy come and celebrate Passover! Now we are slaves, but next year may we be free.

Set down the matzot.

THE FOUR QUESTIONS

Pour the second cup of wine.
(Note that it will be quite a while before it is time to drink.)

It is customary for a young child to recite the four questions.

CHILD:
This night is so different
from other nights!

CHILD:

On other nights we can eat regular bread or matzah.
Tonight we only eat matzah.

On other nights we eat other vegetables.
Tonight we eat bitter herbs.

On other nights we do not have to dip our food at all.
Tonight we dip twice.

On other nights we do not have to sit in a certain way.
Tonight we recline.

*Mah nishtanah ha·**lai**·lah hazeh mikol haleilot!*

*Shebechol haleilot **a**·nu ochelin chametz umatzah.*
*Ha·**lai**·lah hazeh kullo matzah.*

*Shebechol haleilot **a**·nu ochelin sh'ar yerakot.*
*Ha·**lai**·lah hazeh maror.*

*Shebechol haleilot ein **a**·nu matbilin afilu **pa**·am echat.*
*Ha·**lai**·lah hazeh shtei f'amim.*

*Shebechol haleilot **a**·nu ochelin bein yoshevin uvein mesubbin.*
*Ha·**lai**·lah hazeh kul·**la**·nu mesubbin.*

LEADER: The Israelites were slaves to Pharaoh in Egypt, but the LORD, our God, took them out with a strong hand and outstretched arm. If the Holy One had not taken them out from Egypt, then the Jewish people today, their children, and their grandchildren would still be slaves to Pharaoh in Egypt.

PARTICIPANT: Even if we were all wise scholars of the Bible, it would still be important for us to celebrate Passover. Even if we were already familiar with the exodus from Egypt, it would still be worthwhile for us to retell this story of redemption every year.

THE FOUR CHILDREN

LEADER: The Bible instructs Jewish parents to tell their children about the exodus from Egypt at this time of year. All parents should teach their children about salvation and living a life of faith. The Bible lists questions our children may ask, each suggesting a different type of child.

PARTICIPANT: A wise child asks, "What are the testimonies and the statutes and the judgments that the LORD, our God, has commanded you?" (Deuteronomy 6:20). This child is eager to learn. We take the opportunity to teach in greater detail.

PARTICIPANT: A wayward child asks, "What is this service to you?" (Exodus 12:26). By saying "to you," he implies that it is not for him. He excludes himself from the people of faith and redemption, which is a dangerous path.

PARTICIPANT: A simple child asks, "What is this?" (Exodus 13:14). Begin by telling this child how God has saved and redeemed us from bondage.

LEADER: But not every child even knows to ask a question. The responsibility is not on the child to ask; it is on the parent to teach. As the verse commands, "You shall tell your son on that day, saying, 'On account of this that the LORD did for me, taking me out of Egypt'" (Exodus 13:8).

THE PROMISE TO ABRAHAM

LEADER: "Formerly, when you did not know God, you were enslaved to those that by nature are not gods" (Galatians 4:8). Even Abraham's father, Terah, served idols. But the LORD has drawn us near to serve him. "He has delivered us from the domain of darkness and transferred us to the kingdom of his beloved Son" (Colossians 1:13).

LEADER: Blessed is the one who keeps his promise to Israel. Even before captivity began, the Holy One set the time of redemption, as he promised to Abraham:

PARTICIPANT: He said to Abraham, "Know for sure that your offspring will be a stranger in a land that is not theirs; they will serve them and be afflicted for four hundred years. But also, I will bring judgment on the nation that they serve, and afterward, they will go out with great possessions." (Genesis 15:13–14)

LEADER: This promise to Abraham has stood strong for the Jewish people in the past and until today. It was not just the Egyptians who rose up against Israel to put an end to them. In every generation there are those who seek to destroy the Jewish people, but the Holy One always delivers them.

THE STORY OF THE EXODUS

LEADER: A wandering Aramean was my father. And he went down into Egypt and sojourned there, few in number, and there he became a nation, great, mighty, and populous. (Deuteronomy 26:5)

PARTICIPANT: But the people of Israel were fruitful and increased greatly; they multiplied and grew exceedingly strong, so that the land was filled with them. (Exodus 1:7)

LEADER: And the Egyptians treated us harshly and humiliated us and laid on us hard labor. (Deuteronomy 26:6)

PARTICIPANT: They set taskmasters over them to afflict them with heavy burdens. They built for Pharaoh store cities, Pithom and Raamses...They ruthlessly made the people of Israel work as slaves. (Exodus 1:11, 13)

LEADER: Then we cried to the LORD, the God of our fathers, and the LORD heard our voice and saw our affliction, our toil, and our oppression. (Deuteronomy 26:7)

PARTICIPANT: And God heard their groaning, and God remembered his covenant with Abraham, with Isaac, and with Jacob. God saw the people of Israel—and God knew. (Exodus 2:24–25)

LEADER: And the LORD brought us out of Egypt with a mighty hand and an outstretched arm, with great deeds of terror, with signs and wonders. (Deuteronomy 26:8)

PARTICIPANT: For I will pass through the land of Egypt that night, and I will strike all the firstborn in the land of Egypt, both man and beast; and on all the gods of Egypt I will execute judgments: I am the LORD. (Exodus 12:12)

LEADER: These are the ten plagues that the Holy One brought upon the Egyptians in Egypt:

Remove a drop of wine from your cup as each plague is mentioned.

Dam – Blood

Tzefardea – Frogs

Kinnim – Lice

Arov – Swarms / Wild Animals

Dever – Livestock Disease

Shechin – Boils

Barad – Hail

Arbeh – Locusts

Choshech – Darkness

Makkat Bechorot – Death of the Firstborn

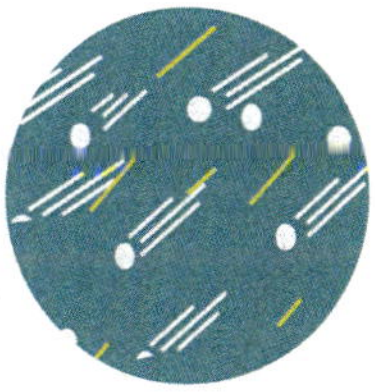

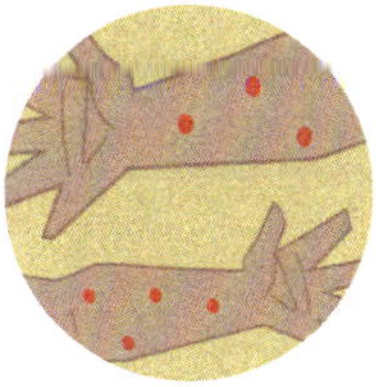

LEADER: The splitting of the sea was an even greater miracle than the ten plagues. The ten plagues in Egypt were called the "finger of God" (Exodus 8:19). But at the parting of the sea, it was not merely a finger but his whole hand:

PARTICIPANT: Israel saw the great [hand] that the LORD used against the Egyptians, so the people feared the LORD, and they believed in the LORD and in his servant Moses. (Exodus 14:31)

DAYENU
(IT WOULD HAVE BEEN ENOUGH)

LEADER: The all-present God has granted us many degrees of goodness in his redemption of Israel!

He took them out from Egypt,
Executed judgment upon the Egyptians,
Executed judgment on their gods,
Killed their firstborn,
Gave Israel their wealth,
Split the sea for them,

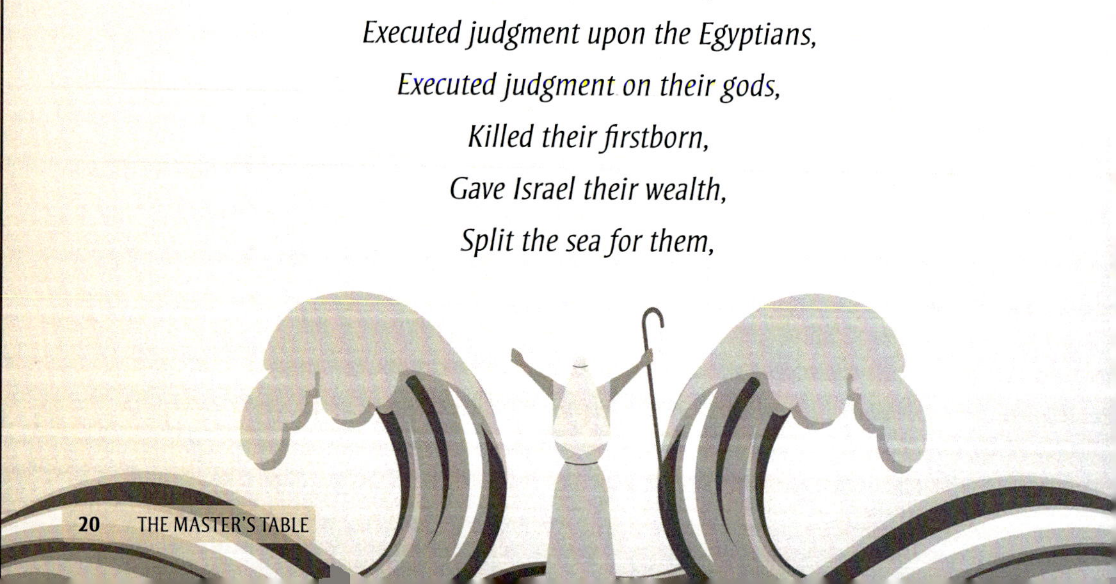

Brought them through on dry ground,

Drowned their enemies in it,

Met their needs in the wilderness for forty years,

Fed them the manna,

Gave them the Sabbath,

Brought them before Mount Sinai,

Gave them the Torah,

Let them enter the land of Israel,

And built for them his Holy Temple, to atone for sin.

LEADER: His Son, Yeshua the Messiah, has granted us so many degrees of kindness!

He came to Israel,

Taught us about his kingdom,

Called us to repentance,

Suffered for our sins,

Died on our behalf,

Rose from the dead,

Ascended to heaven,

Poured out the Spirit,

Drew the nations near to Israel,

Intercedes on our behalf,

Promised to return on the clouds of heaven.

LEADER: Any one of these things would be more than we deserve. *Da·**ye**·nu* — It would have been enough!

THE SYMBOLS OF THE SEDER

LEADER: Rabban Gamliel, under whom the Apostle Paul studied, insisted that no seder is complete unless the following three items are mentioned:

PESACH	MATZAH	MAROR
The Passover Lamb	Unleavened Bread	Bitter Herbs

LEADER: Yeshua taught that Passover commemorates not only the exodus from Egypt, but also our redemption through his suffering, death, and resurrection. Each of these three elements relates in some way to him.

PESACH

THE PASSOVER LAMB

LEADER: When the Israelites were first redeemed from Egypt, they were told to sacrifice a lamb and place its blood on the doorposts of their house. The LORD would see the blood and pass over their homes when he struck the firstborn of the Egyptians.

PARTICIPANT: The Bible commanded the Jewish people to commemorate this through an offering every year at this time. They would take a lamb and slaughter it in the traditional manner and apply the blood to the altar. The meat was roasted and served at the Passover Seder in every generation.

LEADER: Today, in the absence of the Temple, we cannot offer a Passover lamb sacrifice or eat it at our seder, but we use a bone to remind us of the Passover offering.

It would be appropriate at this time to discuss the messianic significance of the Passover offering and how it may serve as a remembrance of the Master. Here are some passages to help with discussion:

1 Corinthians 5:7

Exodus 12:5 | *1 Peter 1:18–19* | *Isaiah 53:7*

Matthew 27:12 | *Exodus 12:46* | *Psalm 34:20*

John 19:33 | *Exodus 12:13* | *Romans 5:9*

MATZAH
UNLEAVENED BREAD

Lift the broken middle matzah.

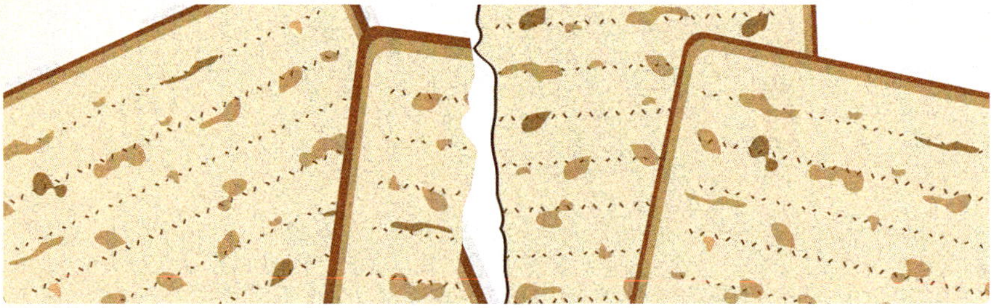

LEADER: When the Holy One revealed himself to Israel and redeemed them, it happened so quickly that there was not enough time for the dough of the Israelites to rise.

PARTICIPANT: The Bible commanded the Jewish people to commemorate this every year by removing all leaven from their homes during the seven days of Passover and eating unleavened bread along with the Passover lamb.

It would be appropriate at this time to discuss the messianic significance of the matzah and how it may serve as a remembrance of the Master. Here are some passages to help with discussion:

1 Corinthians 11:23–24

John 6:51

Luke 12:1

1 Corinthians 5:7–8

MAROR
BITTER HERBS

Return the middle matzah to its place and then lift the bitter herbs.

LEADER: When the Egyptians enslaved the Israelites, they made their lives bitter with suffering in Egypt.

PARTICIPANT: The Bible commanded the Jewish people to commemorate this each year by eating bitter herbs along with the matzah and Passover lamb.

It would be appropriate at this time to discuss the messianic significance of the bitter herbs and how they may serve as a remembrance of the Master. Here are some passages to help with discussion:

Matthew 26:38

1 Peter 2:19

Matthew 26:75

Zechariah 12:10

Set down the bitter herbs.

LEADER: In every generation, a person should see himself as if he had personally gone out from Egypt. As the verse says, "You shall tell your son on that day, saying, 'On account of this that the LORD did for me, taking me out of Egypt" (Exodus 13:8).

PARTICIPANT: It was not merely the Jewish people who were redeemed when Israel went out from Egypt. "But thanks be to God, that you who were once slaves of sin have become obedient from the heart to the standard of teaching to which you were committed, and, having been set free from sin, have become slaves of righteousness" (Romans 6:17–18).

PRAISE

Lift the cup of wine.

LEADER: For this reason, it is our duty to give thanks, to praise, to acclaim, to glorify, to uplift, to honor, to bless, to elevate, and to applaud the one who did all these miracles for our fathers and for us: bringing us out from slavery to freedom, from sorrow to joy, from mourning to festivity, from gloom to bright light, from servitude to redemption. And let us offer him a new song. Hallelujah!

Recite the following passages responsively or in any manner desired. Feel free to include your favorite songs of praise.

PSALM 114

When Israel went out from Egypt, the house of Jacob from a people of strange language, Judah became his sanctuary, Israel his dominion. The sea looked and fled; Jordan turned back. The mountains skipped like rams, the hills like lambs. What ails you,

O sea, that you flee? O Jordan, that you turn back? O mountains, that you skip like rams? O hills, like lambs? Tremble, O earth, at the presence of the Lord, at the presence of the God of Jacob, who turns the rock into a pool of water, the flint into a spring of water.

THE BLESSING OF ZECHARIAH

Blessed be the Lord God of Israel, for he has visited and redeemed his people and has raised up a horn of salvation for us in the house of his servant David, as he spoke by the mouth of his holy prophets from of old, that we should be saved from our enemies and from the hand of all who hate us; to show the mercy promised to our fathers and to remember his holy covenant, the oath that he swore to our father Abraham, to grant us that we, being delivered from the hand of our enemies, might serve him without fear, in holiness and righteousness before him all our days. (Luke 1:68–75)

THE SECOND CUP

LEADER: Blessed are you, O LORD, our God, King of the universe, who creates the fruit of the vine.

*Baruch attah ADONAI elo·***hei***·nu,* **me***·lech ha'olam, borei pri ha·***ga***·fen.*

PARTICIPANTS: Amen.

Lean to the left as you drink the second cup.

⑥ ROCHTZAH

THE SECOND WASHING

It is customary to rinse the hands again in preparation for eating bread.

⑦ MOTZI

THE BLESSING FOR BREAD

Lift the three matzot.

LEADER: We thank you, our Father, for the life and for the knowledge that you made known to us through your servant Yeshua. Yours is the glory forever.

LEADER: Just as this piece of bread was scattered over the mountains and gathered together, so may your assembly be gathered from the ends of the earth into your kingdom. For yours is the glory and the power through Yeshua forever.

LEADER: Blessed are you, O LORD, our God, King of the universe, who brings bread out of the earth.

*Baruch attah ADONAI elo·**hei**·nu, **me**·lech ha'olam, ha·**mo**·tzi **le**·chem min ha·**a**·retz.*

PARTICIPANTS: Amen.

⑧ MATZAH

EATING MATZAH

Set down the bottom matzah, but continue to hold the top and the middle (broken) matzah.

LEADER: Blessed are you who sanctified Israel and commanded them about eating matzah.

PARTICIPANTS: Amen.

LEADER: And he took bread, and when he had given thanks, he broke it and gave it to them, saying, "This is my body, which is given for you. Do this in remembrance of me." (Luke 22:19)

Break apart the top and middle matzot and give each participant a piece from both. If there is not enough for everyone, supplement with additional matzah, but save the bottom piece.

Lean to the left as you eat the matzah.

⑨ MAROR

BITTER HERBS

Take the Romaine lettuce and dip it in charoset.

LEADER: Blessed are you who sanctified Israel and commanded them about eating bitter herbs.

PARTICIPANTS: Amen.

Eat the lettuce, but do not lean.

⑩ KORECH

MATZAH AND BITTER HERBS TOGETHER

Break apart the bottom matzah so that each person gets a piece. If there is not enough for everyone, supplement with additional matzah.

Use the matzah and horseradish or lettuce to make a sandwich. Dip the whole combination in charoset.

LEADER: When the Temple was standing, Hillel the Elder explained that the meat of the Passover lamb, the matzah, and the bitter herbs should all be combined together to fulfill the commandment: "They shall eat it with unleavened bread and bitter herbs" (Numbers 9:11).

Lean to the left as you eat the combination of matzah and bitter herbs.

⑪ SHULCHAN ORECH

THE MEAL IS SERVED

Enjoy the meal. When the participants are finished eating and ready to continue, read the following passage.

LEADER: Jesus, knowing that the Father had given all things into his hands, and that he had come from God and was going back to God, rose from supper. He laid aside his outer garments, and taking a towel, tied it around his waist. Then he poured water into a basin and began to wash the disciples' feet and to wipe them with the towel that was wrapped around him.

PARTICIPANT: When he had washed their feet and put on his outer garments and resumed his place, he said to them, "Do you understand what I have done to you? You call me Teacher and Lord, and you are right, for so I am. If I then, your Lord and Teacher, have washed your feet, you also ought to wash one another's feet. For I have given you an example, that you also should do just as I have done to you. Truly, truly, I say to you, a servant is not greater than his master, nor is a messenger greater than the one who sent him. If you know these things, blessed are you if you do them. (John 13:3–5,12–17)

⑫ TZAFUN

EATING THE HIDDEN MATZAH

Uncover the afikoman, the piece of matzah that was wrapped and set aside at the beginning of the seder.

Break apart the afikoman so that each person gets a piece. If there is not enough for everyone, you can supplement with additional matzah.

One should not eat any other food after the afikoman.

⑬ BARECH

GIVING THANKS FOR THE MEAL

Pour the third cup of wine.

LEADER: Blessed are you, O LORD, our God, King of the universe, who nourishes the entire world with goodness, grace, devotion, and compassion. He gives bread to all flesh, for his devotion is eternal. Because of his great goodness we have never lacked, and we shall never lack nourishment forever and ever. For the sake of his great name, for God provides for and nourishes all, who does good to all and prepares nourishment for all of his creatures which he has made.

LEADER: We thank you, our holy Father, for your holy name that you have caused to dwell in our hearts, and for the knowledge, faithfulness, and eternal life that you have made known to us through your servant Yeshua. Yours is the glory forever.

LEADER: Blessed are you, O LORD, who nourishes all.

PARTICIPANTS: Amen.

LEADER: You, O LORD of Legions, created all things for the sake of your name; you gave nourishment and drink for human beings to enjoy, in order that they would give thanks to you. You also bestowed upon us spiritual nourishment and drink and eternal life through your Servant. And for all things, we thank you because you are powerful. Yours is the glory forever.

PARTICIPANTS: Amen.

LEADER: Remember, O LORD, your congregation to rescue her from all evil, and to make her complete in your love. Our God, let the remembrance of us, of Jerusalem your holy city, of Messiah, son of David, your servant, and of all your people, the house of Israel, ascend, come, and be seen and accepted before you. Take note of these things and grant preservation, goodness, grace, kindness, compassion, life, and peace on this day of the Festival of *Matzot*. For you, our God, are a gracious and compassionate King. Gather the betrothed from the four winds to your kingdom that you have prepared for her. For yours is the power and the glory forever.

PARTICIPANTS: Amen.

LEADER: May grace come and may this world pass away. Hoshana to the God of David! Everyone who is holy, let him come. Everyone who is not, let him repent. Maranatha! Amen.

PARTICIPANTS: Amen.

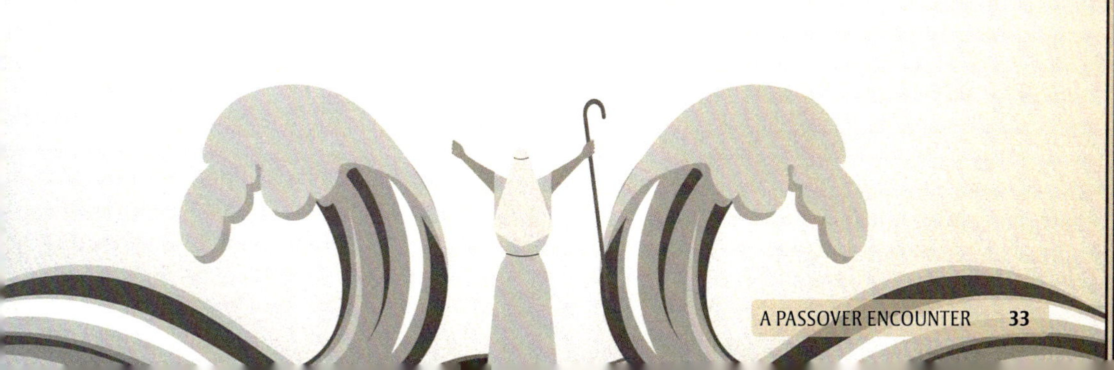

THE THIRD CUP

LEADER: And likewise Jesus took the cup after they had eaten, saying, "This cup that is poured out for you is the new covenant in my blood" (Luke 22:20).

LEADER: Blessed are you, O LORD, our God, King of the universe, who creates the fruit of the vine.

*Baruch attah ADONAI elo·**hei**·nu, **me**·lech ha'olam, borei pri ha·**ga**·fen.*

PARTICIPANTS: Amen.

Lean to the left as you drink the third cup.

THE CUP OF ELIJAH

Pour the fourth cup of wine. Also, fill the cup of Elijah, and open the door to see if Elijah has arrived.

LEADER: Pour out your anger on the nations that do not know you, and on the kingdoms that do not call upon your name! For they have devoured Jacob and laid waste his habitation. (Psalm 79:6–7)

PARTICIPANT: May their camp be a desolation; let no one dwell in their tents. (Psalm 69:25)

PARTICIPANT: You will pursue them in anger and destroy them from under your heavens, O LORD. (Lamentations 3:66)

Close the door.

⑭ HALLEL

PSALMS OF PRAISE

Recite the following passages responsively or in any manner desired. Feel free to include your favorite songs of praise.

PSALM 118

Oh give thanks to the LORD, for he is good; for his steadfast love endures forever! Let Israel say, "His steadfast love endures forever." Let the house of Aaron say, "His steadfast love endures forever." Let those who fear the LORD say, "His steadfast love endures forever."

Out of my distress I called on the LORD; the LORD answered me and set me free. The LORD is on my side; I will not fear. What can man do to me? The LORD is on my side as my helper; I shall look in triumph on those who hate me. It is better to take refuge in the LORD than to trust in man. It is better to take refuge in the LORD than to trust in princes.

All nations surrounded me; in the name of the LORD I cut them off! They surrounded me, surrounded me on every side; in the name of the LORD I cut them off! They surrounded me like bees; they went out like a fire among thorns; in the name of the LORD I cut them off! I was pushed hard, so that I was falling, but the LORD helped me. The LORD is my strength and my song; he has become my salvation.

Glad songs of salvation are in the tents of the righteous: "The right hand of the LORD does valiantly, The right hand of the LORD exalts, the right hand of the LORD does valiantly!" I shall not die, but I shall live, and recount the deeds of the LORD. The LORD has disciplined me severely, but he has not given me over to death.

Open to me the gates of righteousness, that I may enter through them and give thanks to the LORD. This is the gate of the LORD; the righteous shall enter through it. I thank you that you have answered me and have become my salvation. The stone that the builders rejected has become the cornerstone. This is the LORD's doing; it is marvelous in our eyes. This is the day that the LORD has made; let us rejoice and be glad in it.

Save us, we pray, O LORD! O LORD, we pray, give us success!

Blessed is he who comes in the name of the LORD! We bless you from the house of the LORD.

The LORD is God, and he has made his light to shine upon us. Bind the festal sacrifice with cords, up to the horns of the altar! You are my God, and I will give thanks to you; you are my God; I will extol you. Oh give thanks to the LORD, for he is good; for his steadfast love endures forever!

PSALM 136

Give thanks to
the LORD, for he is good, for his steadfast love endures forever.

Give thanks to
the God of gods, for his steadfast love endures forever.

Give thanks to
the Lord of lords, for his steadfast love endures forever;

to him who alone
does great wonders, for his steadfast love endures forever;

to him who by understanding
made the heavens, for his steadfast love endures forever;

to him who spread out
the earth above the waters, for his steadfast love endures forever;

to him who made
the great lights, for his steadfast love endures forever;

the sun
to rule over the day, for his steadfast love endures forever;

the moon and stars
to rule over the night, for his steadfast love endures forever;

to him who struck down
the firstborn of Egypt, for his steadfast love endures forever;

and brought Israel out
from among them, for his steadfast love endures forever;

with a strong hand
and an outstretched arm, for his steadfast love endures forever;

to him who divided
the Red Sea in two, for his steadfast love endures forever;

and made Israel pass
through the midst of it, for his steadfast love endures forever;

but overthrew Pharaoh
and his host in the Red Sea, for his steadfast love endures forever;

to him who led his people
through the wilderness, for his steadfast love endures forever;

to him who struck down
great kings, for his steadfast love endures forever;

and killed mighty kings, for his steadfast love endures forever;

Sihon, king of the Amorites, for his steadfast love endures forever;

and Og, king of Bashan, for his steadfast love endures forever;

and gave their land
as a heritage, for his steadfast love endures forever;

a heritage to Israel his servant, for his steadfast love endures forever.

It is he who remembered us
in our low estate, for his steadfast love endures forever;

and rescued us from our foes, for his steadfast love endures forever;
he who gives food to all flesh, for his steadfast love endures forever.

Give thanks
to the God of heaven, for his steadfast love endures forever.

LEADER: All creation will praise you, O LORD! Let all those you redeemed give thanks, bless, acclaim, glorify, lift up, sanctify, and enthrone your name, our King! It is good to give thanks to you, and it is fitting to make music to your name. From age to age, you are God.

THE FOURTH CUP

LEADER: Blessed are you, O LORD, our God, King of the universe, who creates the fruit of the vine.

*Baruch attah ADONAI elo·**hei**·nu, **me**·lech ha'olam, borei pri ha·**ga**·fen.*

PARTICIPANTS: Amen.

Lean to the left as you drink the fourth cup.

LEADER: Blessed are you, O LORD, our God, King of the universe, for the vine and for the fruit of the vine. Have compassion on Zion, the dwelling place of your glory, and rebuild Jerusalem. "Let us go up to the mountain of the LORD, to the house of the God of Jacob, that he may teach us his ways and that we may walk in his paths. For out of Zion shall go forth the law, and the word of the LORD from Jerusalem" (Isaiah 2:3). Make us glad on this Festival of *Matzot*, for you are good and kind to all. Blessed are you, O LORD, for your kingdom and for the fruit of the vine.

⑮ NIRTZAH

CONCLUSION

LEADER: The seder is complete. Just as we ate and drank together in memory of our Messiah, may we soon eat and drink with him in the kingdom.

LEADER: Pure one who dwells in the heavens above,
Gather together your people in your love.
Soon, take your plantings and lead them along,
Ransomed, to Zion with spirited song.

ALL: Next year in Jerusalem!

*Leshanah haba'ah birusha·**la**·yim!*